CW01512554

A Canvas of Unseen Connections

In shadows where the silence breaks,
Threads of thoughts begin to weave,
Colors blend, and hope awakes,
Artistry in hearts we believe.

Every glance speaks a deep tale,
A brush of souls in fleeting time,
Together we cannot fail,
Harmony is our shared rhyme.

The canvas waits, our hands unite,
With every stroke, we share a dream,
Boundless paths in soft twilight,
A portrait bright, a flowing stream.

Echoes linger in the air,
Whispers dance on gentle breeze,
In the tapestry we share,
Connections bloom like summer trees.

Framed in moments, always near,
Each bond a story etched in light,
In myriad hues, we persevere,
Creating beauty, pure and bright.

Original title:

Serene Trust

Author: Mirell Mesipuu

ISBN HARDBACK: 978-1-80560-209-5

ISBN PAPERBACK: 978-1-80560-674-1

The Murmurs of Soft Devotion

In shadows where the heart yearns,
Gentle whispers tend the flame,
With every sigh, the spirit turns,
In quiet ways, we call your name.

Days unfold in tender grace,
Shadows dance with every breath,
Bonding visions we embrace,
In silence lingers love, not death.

Fingers brush like autumn leaves,
Each moment shared, a vow to keep,
In the stillness, the heart believes,
Soft devotion runs deep and steep.

Through time's passage, love will stay,
Echoing in every tender sound,
Murmurs guide us on our way,
In the warmth of love, we're bound.

Every heartbeat sings the praise,
Of bonds both fierce and gently spun,
In the night, the light displays,
Together, forever as one.

In the Arms of Gentle Whispers

Within the shadows of the night,
Your voice a balm, so soft and kind,
Whispers cradle dreams in flight,
A solace found, two hearts entwined.

Like petals floating through the air,
Each secret shared, a lullaby,
In your embrace, I find my care,
As starlit skies begin to sigh.

The world outside fades from our view,
In sacred stillness, time suspends,
In the arms of love so true,
A realm where every journey mends.

Words like feathers softly fall,
Each sentiment a quiet grace,
In whispers, we can feel it all,
Together in this timeless space.

With each breath, our spirits dance,
A harmony beyond the veil,
In every glance, a sweet romance,
In gentle whispers, we prevail.

Beneath the Canopy of Stars

Underneath the velvet sky,
Where dreams and hopes take flight,
Stars like lanterns floating high,
Guiding hearts through the night.

Moments twinkle, rare and bright,
Every glance a promise made,
In the glow of soft moonlight,
Whispers dance, and fears all fade.

With every breath, the cosmos sighs,
A tapestry of shimmered grace,
In the depth of limitless skies,
Love finds shelter in this space.

Beneath the canopy of fate,
We discover what's meant to be,
In quiet stillness, we await,
A universe that sets us free.

So let us wander, hand in hand,
Among the stars, forevermore,
In the night's enchanting strand,
We'll write our tale upon the shore.

Still Waters Run Deep

In the silence, shadows play,
Reflections dance in soft array.
Beneath the stillness, secrets dwell,
Whispers echo, tales to tell.

Gentle ripples caress the shore,
Each wave speaks of what's in store.
Silent depths, a hidden plea,
The heart knows what's meant to be.

A mirror holds the moon's soft light,
Guiding souls through the night.
In calm, we find the strength to cope,
Still waters cradle dreams and hope.

Beneath the surface, life abounds,
Hidden treasures in the sounds.
Quiet currents sweep away the past,
In tranquil moments, peace is cast.

So pause awhile, let silence breathe,
In stillness, let your spirit weave.
For in the depths, we truly find,
A world of wonder, intertwined.

Unspoken Bonds

In the quiet, hearts align,
Words unspoken, yet divine.
Through a glance, the stories flow,
In the silence, feelings grow.

Hands entwined in shadowed light,
No need for words, the bond feels right.
Eyes that meet in knowing stares,
Unseen threads weave through our cares.

Trust builds in the softest sighs,
A connection that never lies.
Moments shared, though fleeting fast,
In our hearts, these memories last.

The space between, a gentle thread,
Ties the living to the dead.
Unvoiced love, a sacred vow,
In the stillness, we both know how.

Together yet, apart we stand,
Unified by a silent hand.
Beyond the noise, the world can see,
The unspoken love that sets us free.

A Soothing Assurance

In the dawn, a soft embrace,
Warming hearts with gentle grace.
Daylight whispers, worries fade,
In the light, a peace is made.

A simple touch, a knowing smile,
Turns the chaos into style.
In soothing words, we find our peace,
A soft assurance, sweet release.

Like a breeze that sweeps the land,
Tender moments, hand in hand.
Nature sings a timeless tune,
Beneath the sun, beneath the moon.

The burdens lift, the spirits rise,
Through the clouds, we find our skies.
In love's embrace, we find a way,
A soothing promise for each day.

So gather close, let worries part,
In this haven, heal your heart.
Together we can brave the storm,
In the warmth, we find our form.

Beneath the Calm Surface

Underneath a tranquil guise,
Lie the secrets, no disguise.
Still waters hide the storms we've fought,
In the depths, we learn what's taught.

Ripples dance on the placid face,
Yet the heart knows its own pace.
In stillness, questions often rise,
Searching for the truth in lies.

Beneath the calm, a flicker glows,
A silent force that gently flows.
With every breath, the shadows fade,
In the depths, our fears are laid.

Through every trial, we will stand,
In unity, we join our hand.
Let the current guide our way,
Beneath the calm, we find our sway.

So dive deep into the unknown,
In the silence, seeds are sown.
For beneath the calm and the sweep,
Lie the dreams and hopes we keep.

Embraced by Nature's Graces

In the forest's soft embrace,
Where sunlight dances, leaves sway,
Whispers of the wind's sweet song,
Nature's arms hold night and day.

Mountains stand in silent pride,
Rivers flow with tales untold,
Every creature, side by side,
Life unfolds, a story bold.

Petals bloom in colors bright,
Butterflies in gentle flight,
Moments wrapped in warmth and grace,
Nature's love, our pure delight.

Stars awaken in the night,
Moonlight spills on tranquil skies,
In this world, all feels so right,
Heart and soul, nature's ties.

Time slows down beneath the trees,
Every heartbeat finds its place,
In this peace, all worries cease,
Embraced by nature's sweet grace.

Threads of Quiet Assurance

In the stillness of the dawn,
Whispers float on morning air,
Hope unfolds with every yawn,
Faith is woven everywhere.

Gentle hands of fate align,
Casting threads of silver light,
Each connection, by design,
Guides us through the darkest night.

Voices mingle soft and sweet,
Echoes of a timeless truth,
In our hearts, we feel the beat,
Of the bonds that carry youth.

Like a tapestry so fine,
Woven with both joy and pain,
In each stitch, our lives entwine,
Threads of love that still remain.

With each step, assurance grows,
In the dance of fate we trust,
Through the highs and all the lows,
In these threads, we find our must.

The Secret Garden of Loyalty

In a garden, hidden well,
Where the shadows softly play,
Loyalty, a protected spell,
Blossoms bright in soft array.

Whispers linger on the breeze,
Promises held, hearts entwined,
Among the blooms, a quiet ease,
Trust and faith are firmly.bind.

Raindrops glisten on each leaf,
Sunshine mingles, warm and bright,
Here we find our sweet relief,
In this space, the world feels right.

Paths that twist and gently turn,
Lead us deeper into care,
In this haven, love will burn,
Loyalty — a jewel rare.

Every flower tells a tale,
Of a bond that will not break,
In this garden, we prevail,
Together, hearts awake.

Trusting in the Gentle Rain

When the skies begin to weep,
And the earth drinks in each drop,
Trusting in the sound so deep,
Life awakens, roots will pop.

Clouds like blankets softly fall,
Wrapping dreams in shadows gray,
In the rain's sweet, calming call,
Each worry seems to drift away.

Puddles form, reflections shine,
Splashing joy on weary feet,
With each drop, the world aligns,
Nature's rhythm, pure and sweet.

Hope emerges from the ground,
Every raindrop sings its song,
In the silence, peace is found,
Trusting rain will carry on.

Soak in moments, breathe the air,
Let the worries wash away,
In this trust we find repair,
Gentle rain, our soft ballet.

In the Shade of Certainty

In the shade of certainty, we stand,
A world built strong, a steady hand.
Whispers of doubt float like leaves,
Yet rooted in truth, our heart believes.

The sun may wane, the storms may roar,
In this embrace, we seek no more.
Shadows dance, but fears will fade,
For in this place, foundations laid.

Paths may twist, the way unclear,
But comfort blooms, our vision near.
Each breath a promise, gently spoken,
In certainty's arms, the silence broken.

We walk together, side by side,
In the shade of what we cannot hide.
Every step a testament, every sigh,
In this sacred trust, we learn to fly.

Here we linger, as seasons turn,
In the dance of life, our spirits burn.
Though winds may shift and echoes stray,
In the shade of certainty, we choose to stay.

The Unwavering Path

The path unfolds beneath our feet,
With every heartbeat, our souls meet.
Through trials made and lessons learned,
In the fire of life, our passion burned.

Each step a promise, firm and clear,
The road ahead, though paved with fear.
With steadfast hearts, we follow through,
Bound by love, in all we do.

The journey winds, it sways like trees,
Yet in our hearts, a gentle breeze.
Guides us onward, unshakeable force,
Together we move, a destined course.

Through shadows deep and valleys wide,
We journey forth, with hope our guide.
The lantern glows, a beacon's light,
In the unwavering path, we find our flight.

So let the storms come, let them rage,
With courage fierce, we turn the page.
For in our unity, there's strength to laugh,
And in our hearts, the unwavering path.

Unseen Threads

In the tapestry of life, we weave,
Unseen threads, through which we believe.
A gentle tug, a whispered call,
Connecting us all, threading through each wall.

Woven moments, both near and far,
A fabric rich, each story, a star.
Some threads pull tight, while others roam,
In this great design, we find our home.

Invisible bonds, they tie us close,
In laughter shared and silent prose.
Each encounter, a stitch in time,
Unseen threads weave love's sweet rhyme.

Through the chaos, the colors blend,
Patterns emerge, the patterns mend.
In the silence, a symphony sounds,
A dance of life, where truth abounds.

So let us cherish, these threads we find,
In every heart, a story lined.
For together we stand, though often blurred,
By unseen threads, our fates conferred.

The Mellow Assurance

In the mellow assurance of the day,
Soft whispers soothe, carry worries away.
Golden rays dance on the calm sea,
In quiet grace, we learn to be free.

With every sunset, colors unfold,
A tranquil promise, a story retold.
Embraced in warmth, we let time flow,
In mellow assurance, our spirits grow.

Through gentle laughter, we find our space,
In shared moments, a soft embrace.
The world may rush, but here we stand,
In the mellow assurance, hand in hand.

Unrushed rhythms guide our way,
With every heartbeat, a brand new day.
In the calm of dusk, we breathe in deep,
In the mellow assurance, our dreams we keep.

So let us wander, where shadows play,
In the tender twilight, we find our way.
For in this softness, love's embrace,
The mellow assurance, our perfect place.

Whispers of Calm Assurance

In the gentle hush of night,
Softly comes the light,
A promise held so dear,
In shadows, it draws near.

The breeze carries a tune,
Beneath the silver moon,
Where worries fade away,
And hope begins to stay.

Each heartbeat whispers peace,
As doubts begin to cease,
The stars align above,
In an embrace of love.

Through trials, we shall find,
A strength, forever kind,
In every breath we take,
A bond we will not break.

In stillness, we take flight,
Guided by inner light,
With faith as our guide,
Together, we abide.

Beneath the Timid Sky

Draped in hues of gray,
The clouds begin to sway,
A whisper lingers near,
In silence, we hold dear.

The drops begin to fall,
A gentle, soothing call,
Each raindrop sings a song,
A melody so strong.

Through shadows, light will creep,
In valleys, peace we reap,
With every tear that lands,
We rise, hand in hand.

As daylight breaks the gloom,
Bringing promise to bloom,
Each moment shared will last,
In the present, the past.

So let the storm roll by,
For beneath the timid sky,
A brighter day will break,
With every step we take.

The Gentle Embrace of Faith

In the quiet of our hearts,
Faith whispers, never parts,
A beacon shining bright,
Guiding us through the night.

With every breath we draw,
We cherish hope's soft law,
And know, come what may,
Together, we will stay.

In storms, we find our strength,
Measured in love's great length,
Through trials, we will stand,
United, hand in hand.

The dusk will yield to dawn,
With faith, we carry on,
Each step a dance of grace,
In this sacred space.

So let your spirit soar,
With faith forevermore,
For in every embrace,
There's beauty, there's grace.

In Quiet Reliance

Amidst the chaos loud,
We find calm in the crowd,
In whispers soft, we seek,
Comfort in every peak.

The world spins ever fast,
Yet we embrace the last,
Of fleeting moments shared,
In hearts, we are unscared.

With trust, we face the fray,
And forge a brand new way,
In quiet reliance found,
Together, safe and sound.

Each step becomes a song,
Where we both belong,
With every breath we take,
A path we will not break.

So let the whispers flow,
In calm, let our love grow,
In unity, we'll find,
A peace that's intertwined.

The Sun's Warm Gaze on Trusting Hearts

The sun rises bright, a golden hue,
Its warmth wraps around, tender and true.
In trusting hearts, shadows take flight,
Embracing the dawn, igniting the light.

Through laughter and tears, we stand side by side,
With hope as our anchor, love as our guide.
In moments of doubt, we find our way,
With the sun's warm gaze, we greet new day.

Each whisper of wind, a gentle caress,
In trust, we find peace, we find our rest.
With every heartbeat, a promise is made,
In the light of the sun, our fears start to fade.

So let us embrace the journey we take,
With trusted companions, our spirits awake.
For in every sunrise, lies a brand new start,
A testament to love, in each trusting heart.

Tides of Unwavering Faith

The ocean waves crash, relentless and free,
Tides of faith rise, as vast as the sea.
In moments of struggle, we stand with might,
Trusting the journey will lead us to light.

With each ebb and flow, our spirits will soar,
Through storms and calms, we shall seek more.
In the depths of despair, hope is our sail,
Guiding us forward, though sometimes we fail.

Unwavering faith, a beacon of grace,
In the heart of the storm, we find our place.
With every cresting wave, our fears drift away,
The tides remind us, we'll be okay.

Let us ride the currents, hand in hand,
Through trials and triumphs, together we stand.
In the rhythm of life, we dance and we sway,
With tides of faith leading the way.

The Peaceful Path Ahead

The path ahead lies quiet and clear,
With whispers of hope, we silence our fear.
As footsteps echo on the soft, cool ground,
A journey of peace in each moment found.

Alongside the trees, we walk in warm light,
With gratitude glowing, our hearts feel so bright.
In the simplicity of nature's embrace,
We find our direction, we find our place.

The rustle of leaves sings sweet melodies,
A chorus of comfort, a gentle breeze.
Each step that we take, a promise to keep,
The peaceful path calls, our spirits leap.

With every sunrise, a brand new start,
A canvas of hope, a work of art.
In harmony moving, let's cherish the day,
On this peaceful path, we forever stay.

A Haven of Hidden Strength

In the depths of silence, strength starts to bloom,
A haven of courage, breaking the gloom.
With whispers of power, we rise from the fall,
Together we stand, united we call.

From roots that run deep, our spirits entwine,
In moments of doubt, our hearts will align.
Each challenge we face, a lesson in grace,
In this haven of strength, we find our place.

Through trials and storms, our essence reveals,
The hidden resilience that our spirit feels.
In the heart of the struggle, we'll find our song,
Together we flourish, together we're strong.

With every heartbeat, our stories unfold,
In this haven built, our spirits are bold.
So let us embrace the strength that we own,
In this place of refuge, we'll never be alone.

Trusting the River's Flow

The river winds with gentle grace,
Through valleys deep and open space.
It knows the path, the bends, the turns,
Within its flow, a lesson burns.

Reflections dance on waters bright,
Beneath the sun, a sparkling sight.
With every ripple, life will show,
The strength in trusting where to go.

Along its banks, the willows sway,
In harmony, they find their way.
Together strong, they face the storm,
In every twist, a chance to form.

A current sings a soothing tune,
Under the watchful, watchful moon.
Embrace the path, let shadows blend,
For every river has an end.

So lay your doubts upon the shore,
And trust the river evermore.
With open hearts, we can explore,
The endless journey we adore.

The Calm Before the Dawn

The night descends, a velvet cloak,
As silence stirs, the shadows choke.
Stars twinkle bright, the world in repose,
In whispered dreams, the spirit grows.

With closed eyes, we await the light,
A crisp embrace of the coming sight.
The stillness hums, a breath held tight,
In moments soft, we feel the night.

The echoes fade, a pulse so strong,
A lullaby, as if a song.
Each heartbeat slows, prepares the way,
For golden rays to greet the day.

As dawn creeps close, the colors blend,
Kissing the horizon, light will send.
We stand in awe with hearts anew,
The calm before brings hope into view.

So cherish this tranquil embrace,
This fleeting time, this sacred space.
For as the dawn begins to glow,
We greet the world, the seeds we sow.

Embers of Hope in the Stillness

In the quiet, embers spark,
Glowing softly in the dark.
Hope ignites with every breath,
A flicker defying death.

Through the silence, whispers rise,
Carrying dreams to painted skies.
Gentle warmth within our souls,
Even as the shadow rolls.

Beneath the weight of night's embrace,
Hope persists with tender grace.
Each ember tells a tale of light,
That fights against the creeping night.

As stars reflect on waters clear,
We hold our wishes close and near.
For even in the darkest hours,
Our hearts still bloom with radiant flowers.

So let the embers softly glow,
A beacon lit through highs and lows.
In stillness, find the strength to cope,
For life shall rise from shards of hope.

A Garden of Birdsong's Promises

In a garden, flowers sway,
As melodies bloom day by day.
The songbirds greet the morning bright,
Voices mingling, pure delight.

Their joyful tunes weave through the air,
A symphony beyond compare.
Each note a promise, sweet and clear,
That sings of love and casts out fear.

Beneath the boughs, where shadows play,
Life awakens in bright array.
With every chirp, the heart takes flight,
In harmony, the world ignites.

Petals open, colors bold,
While stories of the day unfold.
In every rustle, there's a chance,
To join the birds in nature's dance.

So come and tread this vibrant ground,
Where every heart can feel unbound.
In gardens lush, with songs so sweet,
We find our place, our lives complete.

Mosaics of Unbreakable Bonds

In the fabric of time, threads intertwine,
Colors of love, in harmony, they shine.
Each moment a piece, a story unfolds,
A tapestry woven, the warmth it holds.

Through storms we weather, hand in hand we stand,
Shining our light, like grains of sand.
Together as one, we journey through night,
Mosaics of memories, forever bright.

With laughter as glue, and tears as the paint,
Every scar a blessing, no room for restraint.
The heartbeats align, in rhythm and grace,
A masterpiece crafted, no time can erase.

In silence we speak, our spirits entwined,
Echoes of trust, in kindness defined.
Anchored in love, we flourish and grow,
These unbreakable bonds, forever we'll sow.

The Cuddle of Hope in Dawn's Light

As dawn stretches wide, with colors so bright,
Whispers of hope, like stars in the night.
The world awakens, a soft gentle sigh,
In the cuddle of warmth, even shadows comply.

Golden rays dance, on each tender leaf,
Promises linger, a sweet, soft belief.
In the hush of the morn, our dreams take their flight,
Wrapped in the glow, we embrace the new light.

With every heartbeat, new chances arise,
A canvas of moments, painted with skies.
In the cuddle of dawn, all burdens release,
Hope's gentle embrace, a sweet, quiet peace.

Together we rise, with hearts open wide,
In the arms of this day, let love be our guide.
In every new sunrise, our spirits ignite,
A dance of unyielding, in dawn's gentle light.

Lullabies in the Language of Trust

Softly I sing, in whispers sincere,
Lullabies cradle, silence draws near.
With words like feathers, they float in the air,
In the language of trust, we share what we care.

With every note, a promise is made,
A symphony sweet, that never will fade.
Each heart is a drum, in perfect time,
Together we create, a melodious rhyme.

When shadows creep close, and doubts start to rise,
In the hush of our song, we look to the skies.
For trust is the bridge, that carries us through,
In lullabies sung, our dreams feel anew.

Let go of the fears, let the music flow,
In the language of trust, our hearts deeply know.
With every refrain, together we soar,
In this tender embrace, we'll always explore.

Hushed Reveries of Mutual Faith

In quiet corners, our hopes intertwine,
Hushed reveries whisper, so gentle, divine.
With eyes closed tight, we dream side by side,
In the warmth of our faith, we choose not to hide.

Fingers entwined, in the stillness we stand,
Carving our path, with love's guiding hand.
Every heartbeat echoes, a truth that we know,
In mutual faith, our spirits will glow.

With each subtle sigh, the world fades away,
In the hush of this moment, we silently sway.
With trust as our anchor, and dreams as our guide,
Together we flourish, with nothing to bide.

These hushed reveries, where our souls find release,
In the tranquil embrace, we discover our peace.
With whispers of hope, and dreams softly spun,
In mutual faith, our journey's begun.

Whispers of Faith

In the still of the night, whispers arise,
Softly they carry, like stars in the skies.
Hope dances lightly on each gentle breeze,
Faith weaves a pattern, our hearts' quiet ease.

In challenges faced, shadows may loom,
Yet light finds a way to dispel any gloom.
Each step we take, grounded in trust,
Guided by whispers, our hearts learn to rust.

The journey unfolds, a path yet untold,
With courage ignited, our spirits behold.
The whispers of faith, a melody sweet,
In the silence of doubt, our hearts find their beat.

Hands joined together, we stand side by side,
In moments of doubt, our dreams still abide.
Through valleys of shadows, we find our way,
Whispers of faith guiding night into day.

With every heartbeat, a promise we make,
To nurture the flame, for our souls' gentle sake.
Life's tapestry woven with colors so bright,
In whispers of faith, we discover our light.

A Gentle Embrace

In the arms of the dawn, sun softly gleams,
A gentle embrace, like the warmest of dreams.
Clouds drift away, unveiling the sky,
With love all around, we learn how to fly.

In each tender moment, we find our place,
Wrapped in compassion, no need to chase.
The warmth of a smile, shared glances so bright,
Each heartbeat a promise, each lullaby light.

Through storms that may rage and seasons that change,
In this gentle embrace, our souls rearrange.
Together we stand, through thick and through thin,
In life's endless dance, we both strive to win.

The beauty of silence, the language we speak,
In kindness and patience, we find what we seek.
In moments of sorrow, joy dances in place,
Holding on tightly, we cherish the grace.

With gratitude whispered, we nurture our dreams,
In the gentle embrace of love's flowing streams.
Each heartbeat a rhythm, each tear a release,
In our dance of affection, we find sweet peace.

The Quiet Assurance

In the hush of the night, a whisper remains,
A quiet assurance that love never wanes.
Stars hang like lanterns, guiding our way,
In the stillness of time, our worries give way.

Through trials we face, doubts clouding our mind,
There's strength in the silence, a solace to find.
In each gentle moment, we gather our dreams,
Trusting that life flows in delicate streams.

The dawn brings a promise, a chance to renew,
With hope as our anchor, we tread upon dew.
The heart knows its journey, though paths may be steep,
In quiet assurance, our faith runs deep.

We carry within us the light of our truth,
In the shadows of doubt, we embrace our youth.
With courage ignited, each step we must take,
In the quiet assurance, our spirits awake.

With love as our compass, we march ever on,
For in every heartbeat, a new day is drawn.
The quiet assurance of dreams held so tight,
Guides us from darkness and into the light.

Foundations of Harmony

In the heart of the world, foundations are laid,
Brick by brick, building dreams unafraid.
With laughter and love, we craft our abode,
Foundations of harmony, where peace is bestowed.

Through challenges faced, we stand hand in hand,
Each moment a lesson, a chance to expand.
In the warmth of compassion, we resonate strong,
Harmonies blending, a beautiful song.

With kindness as roots, we grow ever taller,
Together we rise, our spirits don't falter.
Each voice is a note in this symphony wide,
Foundations of harmony, with joy as our guide.

Through storms that may batter, our strength won't betray,

In the dance of our lives, we find our own way.
Bound by affection, our hearts interlace,
Creating a tapestry filled with grace.

In the echoes of time, let our laughter resound,
For in unity's heartbeat, true love can be found.
In foundations of harmony, together we thrive,
With hope in our hearts, forever alive.

A Pathway Through the Mist

In the morning's gentle haze,
Footsteps whisper on the trail.
Each breath a promise made,
As shadows of doubt begin to pale.

Veils of fog begin to break,
Revealing secrets of the day.
With every cautious step I take,
The path guides me on my way.

Nature's songs hum in the air,
A melody soft and pure.
In this stillness, I find care,
For the journey, I endure.

As the sun begins to rise,
Light dances on the trees.
Hope awakens in the skies,
Carried softly on the breeze.

With each moment, I embrace,
The beauty in the unknown.
In the mist, I find my place,
A pathway through seeds I've sown.

Soft Murmurs of Eternal Promises

In the quiet of the night,
Whispers weave through the dark.
Each sound a gentle light,
Igniting the faithful spark.

Promises float on the air,
Beneath the shimmering stars.
Moments linger, soft and rare,
Healing all of life's scars.

Time flows like a soothing stream,
Carving paths through rocky ground.
In dreams, we softly beam,
Where true love can be found.

Every vow, a tender note,
Played on heartstrings with grace.
Together we learn and float,
In this wondrous, sacred space.

So let these murmurs ignite,
A flame that will ever hold.
In the dark, we find our light,
Soft promises, brave and bold.

Where Trust Grows Like Ancient Trees

In a grove of timeless grace,
Roots entwined beneath the ground.
Each branch, a warm embrace,
In their shade, we are found.

Leaves whisper secrets in the breeze,
Telling tales of strength and time.
Here, in peace, my spirit frees,
With every heartbeat, I climb.

Barks worn by the passage years,
Mark the trials we have faced.
From each ring, wisdom appears,
In this sanctuary, embraced.

Sunlight filters through the limbs,
Casting patterns on the floor.
In the warmth, my heart now swims,
Trust grows deeply, evermore.

Together, we will rise and sway,
In harmony, side by side.
Where trust grows like trees each day,
In this bond, we shall abide.

Sails Raised in Quiet Confidence

In the harbor, calm and still,
Waves caress the sturdy bows.
With a heart, resolved and will,
Our journey starts, here and now.

Sails unfurl to catch the wind,
Harnessing dreams yet to soar.
With each gust, fresh hopes rescind,
The shore that we leave for more.

Horizons stretch, vast and bright,
A canvas ready for our mark.
Guided by the stars at night,
We set forth from the dark.

In this quiet, fierce embrace,
Confidence lifts us high.
With each wave, we find our pace,
As our spirits learn to fly.

Adventure whispers in our ear,
A call to worlds yet unknown.
With sails raised, we conquer fear,
Together, never alone.

Glimpses of Eternity within Each Other

In the silence, whispers play,
Reflecting dreams that drift away.
In every gaze, a story flows,
A timeless bond that gently grows.

Moments linger, hearts aligned,
In tangled fates, our souls entwined.
Through laughter shared and sorrows deep,
Eternity's promise, ours to keep.

The starlit skies, they guide our way,
In every heartbeat, night and day.
As shadows dance beneath the moon,
We find our truth, a sacred tune.

In quiet hours, secrets unfold,
Stories whispered, yet untold.
Each glance a glimpse of endless time,
In echoes soft, our hearts do rhyme.

Together we weave a tapestry,
Of dreams and hopes, a memory.
In every touch, our worlds collide,
Glimpses of eternity, side by side.

The Slumber of Shared Secrets

In the hush of night, we confide,
Beneath the stars, our thoughts abide.
The moon a witness to our trust,
In whispered tones, it feels a must.

Each secret held like fragile glass,
In silence shared, we let them pass.
The weight of words, so soft and light,
In slumber's arms, we hold them tight.

In gentle dreams, our fears dissolve,
As trust enfolds and hearts evolve.
Through shadows cast, we find the light,
In shared secrets, we take flight.

A quiet pact beneath the stars,
In hidden truths, we heal our scars.
Together we drift, no need to speak,
In this silent slumber, we feel unique.

A bond forged in the still of night,
In shared whispers, everything feels right.
In dreams we weave our stories bold,
The slumber of secrets, forever told.

Walking among Blossoms of Belief

In gardens bright, where petals sway,
We walk the path, come what may.
Each blossom whispers tales of hope,
In vibrant hues, we learn to cope.

Amidst the blooms, our spirits soar,
With every step, we seek for more.
The fragrance sweet, a guiding breeze,
In blossoms of belief, we find ease.

Beneath the sun, our worries fade,
In nature's embrace, we unafraid.
Walking hand in hand, we find our way,
In the dance of color, we choose to stay.

Each petal kissed by morning dew,
A testament to dreams we pursue.
Among the blossoms, fears we release,
In vibrant colors, we find peace.

Together we wander, hearts aglow,
In a world of magic, we let love flow.
Walking among blossoms, we believe,
In every moment, love's reprieve.

A Hearth of Calm Reflections

In the corner, embers glow,
A haven where warm thoughts flow.
With gentle flames, our stories rise,
In quiet moments, truth implies.

The crackling wood sings soft and low,
As shadows dance in evening's show.
In every flicker, memories sway,
A hearth of calm, where fears decay.

We gather close, hearts intertwined,
With whispered dreams, the past defined.
In glowing warmth, our spirits mend,
A place of solace, where hearts blend.

Reflections cast on walls of grace,
In every glance, we find our place.
With voices hushed, we speak of love,
A sacred bond, blessed from above.

In the twilight's glow, we share our fears,
With stories laced in laughter and tears.
A hearth of calm, where time suspends,
In these cherished moments, love transcends.

The Assured Whisper of Tomorrow

In the dawn's light, hopes unfold,
Whispers softly, stories told.
Each heartbeat, a step we take,
In tomorrow's arms, we awake.

Clouds part ways, the sun will shine,
Promises linger, fate align.
With every breath, a chance to grow,
Guided by the warm, sweet glow.

Through trials faced and shadows cast,
We find our strength, resolve steadfast.
Holding dreams close, never sway,
In the assured whisper of the day.

As stars above begin to fade,
New chances bloom in life's parade.
Let not fear silence the song,
For tomorrow's light will keep us strong.

Each moment treasured, never lost,
For every rainbow bears a cost.
Yet love endures, our spirits soar,
In the whispered promise of evermore.

A Tapestry of Gently Woven Dreams

In twilight's embrace, dreams take flight,
Colors swirl in soft moonlight.
Threads of hope, delicate and fine,
Woven together, they intertwine.

A whisper drifts on the evening air,
Dreams unfold, light as a prayer.
In the fabric of night, stories gleam,
We dance in the realm of silent dreams.

Hope's gentle hands, they stitch and sew,
A tapestry rich, where wishes grow.
Each moment savored, a vibrant seam,
Crafting life's most cherished theme.

With every heartbeat, the loom does spin,
Binding our fates, where dreams begin.
In soft shadows, our visions weave,
A kaleidoscope of all we believe.

Awake at dawn, as threads align,
Life's masterpiece, a gift divine.
In the warmth of the morning sun,
We carry the dreams, we have spun.

When Dreams Kiss Reality

In twilight's glow, hopes arise,
Whispers dance in the night skies.
Moments where wishes intertwine,
Where shadows fade, and hearts align.

A bridge of light between the two,
Painted skies, a vibrant hue.
In every heartbeat, dreams unfold,
Promises shared, stories told.

The dawn reveals what dreams can be,
A tapestry of life's journey.
When fantasy meets the morning sun,
A new adventure has begun.

Eyes alight with wonder's glow,
In reality's arms, dreams flow.
With every step, the world we chase,
In the dance of time, we find our place.

As night surrenders to day's embrace,
Dreams become our lasting grace.
In this union, we dare to trust,
To chase the dreams, it's a must.

Anchors in the Flowing Stream

Through currents swift, we seek the shore,
Finding strength in what we adore.
With every wave, we hold on tight,
Anchors tethered, hearts alight.

Life's ebb and flow, we ride the tide,
Together strong, we will abide.
In depths of change, we seek our way,
Guided by stars that never sway.

As moments drift, we stand as one,
In rhythms timed, our work not done.
With love our anchor, ever true,
Through stormy seas, we'll break on through.

Each ripple sings of hope anew,
Flowing together, our bond is due.
Where waters merge, we find our dream,
Anchored firmly in life's great stream.

So let the currents gently sway,
We'll seek the dawn of each new day.
With every heartbeat, we have the grace,
To navigate through time and space.

A Symphony of Gentle Assurances

In quiet tones, the heart's refrain,
Soft melodies in joy and pain.
Each note a touch, a soothing balm,
In life's chaos, a gentle calm.

The harmonies weave through the air,
Notes of comfort, a tender care.
With every chord, we find our way,
Illuminating the darkest day.

Together we rise in rhythmic grace,
In every heartbeat, a sacred space.
The symphony plays, our spirits soar,
In every moment, love's encore.

With whispered words that intertwine,
Resonating, a space divine.
In laughter and tears, we find our song,
In the music of life, we all belong.

So let the orchestra play tonight,
A symphony swathed in soft light.
In each shared silence, we will see,
The beauty of gentle harmony.

The Breath of Safe Understanding

In hushed whispers, hearts confide,
With open arms, we stand beside.
In the quiet, we know the truth,
Life's gentle lessons, eternal youth.

The warmth of eyes that deeply see,
Beyond the words, just you and me.
In every breath, we draw in trust,
In shared silence, we must adjust.

The world outside can push and pull,
Yet here, our bond is always full.
In the comfort of understanding's grace,
We find our pace, our sacred space.

With every sigh, a promise to hold,
In the air, we find stories told.
Together we breathe, hearts intertwined,
In the embrace of a love defined.

So let us cherish this sacred air,
In breaths of hope, we always care.
In safe understanding, we shall rise,
With love and trust, we touch the skies.

A Still Haven of Belief

In quiet corners of the mind,
A refuge where dreams unwind.
Whispers of hope, softly told,
Crafting warmth in the cold.

Through the storms that life may bring,
Resilience weaves a gentle string.
Each thread a promise, bright and clear,
In this haven, have no fear.

Flickering candles, soft and bright,
Guiding souls through the dark night.
A tapestry of faith and love,
Woven gently from above.

With every step, the heart will soar,
Knowing there's always something more.
A quiet strength, a steadfast hand,
Together we will make our stand.

In this stillness, let us believe,
In every moment, we shall achieve.
For in the calm, our spirits find,
A still haven of the heart and mind.

The Soft Glow of Understanding

In the silence, you find your way,
A gentle light leads the sway.
Questions linger, looking deep,
In thoughts that dare to seek.

Through the shadows, wisdom flows,
In every heart, compassion grows.
With kindness shared, we learn to see,
The soft glow in you and me.

Each moment holds a world unknown,
Where seeds of patience are sown.
Together, we bridge the divide,
In the warmth of hearts open wide.

Voices blend, a symphony,
Echoing love's simplicity.
Hand in hand, we walk this road,
With understanding as our code.

So let us cherish this gentle light,
That teaches us to be polite.
In the soft glow, we find our way,
Understanding paves the day.

Where Sails Meet the Breeze

Upon the waters, dreams set free,
Where sails meet the gentle breeze.
A journey whispers through the night,
Guided by the stars so bright.

Waves dance softly, a lullaby,
As horizons expand and fly.
Adventure calls with each new dawn,
In every heart, a hope reborn.

With laughter shared on open seas,
Time flows easy, like summer leaves.
Together we chase the setting sun,
In the rhythm of life, we are one.

The wind carries tales of the brave,
Of souls unbroken by the wave.
In every gust, a promise sings,
That freedom comes on silver wings.

So let your spirit find its course,
Sailing forth with gentle force.
For in this dance, so wild and grand,
We find our place, we take our stand.

Shadows of Gentle Certainty

In the twilight, shadows play,
Softly whispering end of day.
Certainty wrapped in quiet grace,
Finding solace in this space.

The night unfolds its tender light,
Guiding dreams through soft moonlight.
Each star a beacon, shining bright,
Filling hearts with sweet delight.

With every breath, the world feels near,
In shadows cast, we shed our fear.
A gentle touch, a knowing glance,
In shared moments, we find our chance.

Every thought a flickering flame,
Burning steady, yet never the same.
In the quiet, we carve our path,
Finding joy in love's sweet math.

So let us walk this winding road,
With hands entwined, we share the load.
In the shadows, we stand true,
Gentle certainty guiding us through.

Beneath the Canopy of Belief

Shade of dreams above us, wide,
Roots of hope run deep inside.
Whispers of the ancient trees,
Guide our souls like gentle breeze.

In the silence, truth will rise,
Bathed in warmth of sunny skies.
Each leaf tells a story bright,
Beneath the canopy of light.

Together, hand in hand we stand,
In this sacred, trusted land.
Hearts entwined, forever strong,
In harmony, we sing our song.

When the shadows loom and fade,
Through the storms, our bond is made.
Underneath that bough we lay,
In belief, we find our way.

With every rustle, every sigh,
Mounting tides of dreams fly high.
Beneath the canopy we breathe,
In unity, we shall believe.

A Dance in the Light

With open arms, we embrace the dawn,
In every heartbeat, a new song.
Light cascades in golden streams,
In this moment, we dance our dreams.

Chasing shadows, letting go,
With each twirl, our spirits flow.
Laughter echoes through the air,
A melody beyond compare.

Swirling in the morning glow,
With every step, our love will grow.
The world spins in a gentle sway,
Together, we shall find our way.

In this dance, our souls unite,
Two hearts bound in pure delight.
Every movement, pure and free,
A dance in light, just you and me.

As the day turns into night,
We hold on tight, the future bright.
In the rhythm of each breath,
We dance with life, defying death.

Close Eyes, Open Hearts

Close your eyes, let the world fade,
In this moment, love is made.
Open hearts, a bond so true,
In silence, I find you.

In dreams, we wander hand in hand,
Exploring realms that understand.
The language spoken needs no words,
Just the essence of two birds.

With every beat, our spirits soar,
In unity, we ask for more.
Together, facing every spark,
In the light, we leave a mark.

Eyes are closed, yet vision's clear,
With open hearts, we lose our fear.
A dance of trust, a leap of faith,
In this embrace, we find our place.

Close your eyes, feel the grace,
In this moment, our sacred space.
With open hearts, our souls align,
In love's embrace, forever shine.

The Harmony of Trusting Hearts

In whispered secrets, trust is grown,
Two souls join, no longer alone.
Through trials faced and storms endured,
The bond between us feels assured.

In every glance, a silent vow,
To stand together, here and now.
Hearts in sync beneath the stars,
In this dance, we heal old scars.

When life's melodies seem to clash,
We find our rhythm, love's sweet flash.
In the harmony, we learn to share,
Every burden, every prayer.

With trusting hearts, we face the night,
Guided by love's soft light.
In every heartbeat, every sigh,
A symphony that will not die.

Together we create a sound,
In every laugh, our hope is found.
In the space where dreams are birthed,
The harmony of trusting hearts.

Where Light Meets Trust

In the dawn's early embrace,
Whispers of courage unfold,
A promise in every space,
Shimmering dreams like gold.

Beneath the skies of blue,
Hearts dance in a gentle sway,
With hope, we push on through,
Finding strength in light's play.

Each moment, a tender thread,
Woven into our shared fate,
Together where shadows tread,
In trust, we cultivate.

As stars peek through the night,
Guiding paths intertwine,
With every step, a spark of light,
An unbreakable design.

In silence, our spirits sing,
A melody pure and bright,
With every joy we bring,
In harmony, we find delight.

Currents of Gentle Serenity

Upon the river's soft sigh,
Peace flows like a calming stream,
Nature's breath, a lullaby,
Cradled in a tender dream.

Whispers of leaves in the breeze,
Echoes of tranquility's call,
In moments such as these,
We rise, we float, we fall.

Time dances on rippled waves,
As sunlight kisses the shore,
Each heartbeat quietly saves,
The beauty we all adore.

Through valleys, we journey far,
Guided by the stars above,
In stillness, we'll find who we are,
Embraced by nature's love.

With every glance at the sky,
A promise of peace is near,
In currents where heartbeats lie,
Serenity holds us dear.

Petals on the Still Waters

Gently they drift and sway,
Petals soft as a sigh,
Floating in nature's play,
Underneath the wide sky.

Mirrored in calm embrace,
Reflections of beauty gleam,
A moment time won't erase,
Flowing gentle as a dream.

Where the lilies bloom bright,
Colors dance in sweet delight,
Painting the world with light,
In this serene twilight.

Ripples whisper secrets old,
Tales of love, pure and true,
In their silence, stories told,
Petals carry me to you.

As dusk wraps around the day,
A symphony softly plays,
With grace, we'll find our way,
In nature's warm embrace.

The Language of Soft Affection

In the quiet of the night,
Words unspoken find their way,
Hearts converse in soft light,
Love's gentle tune at play.

Each glance, a sweet caress,
A touch, a warm embrace,
In silence, we confess,
Finding joy in this space.

With laughter, we weave dreams,
A tapestry rich and bright,
In the flow of love's streams,
Every star feels just right.

Through whispers, our souls dance,
A rhythm that feels like home,
In moments of sweet romance,
In love, we freely roam.

As dawn breaks, hope will rise,
In the warmth of morning's glow,
In each other's cherished eyes,
Forever, our hearts will know.

Soft Footsteps on Dew-Kissed Grass

Beneath the dawn, a gentle hush,
Whispers through the foliage, a soft rush.
Each step taken, a tender grace,
Morning's breath, a warm embrace.

Sunlight dances on blades of green,
Nature's canvas, a tranquil scene.
With every footfall, a story told,
A tapestry of memories, pure and bold.

The dew collects in crystal beads,
A fleeting moment, the heart concedes.
In every drop, a dream takes flight,
Awakening hopes in the softest light.

Pathways woven with gentle sighs,
Underneath the vast, open skies.
In this stillness, the soul finds peace,
Soft footsteps linger, never cease.

With every pause, the world unfolds,
Nature's secrets, timeless and old.
On dew-kissed grass, we dance and play,
Embracing morning's tender sway.

Echoes of Resilient Hearts

In shadows cast by doubt's cruel hand,
The heart beats strong, a steadfast band.
With every echo, hope takes flight,
Resilient dreams glow through the night.

Through storms that rage and winds that howl,
Faith stands firm, an unwavering prowl.
Each lesson learned, a treasure grows,
In the depth of struggle, true love flows.

Whispers of courage fill the air,
A symphony of strength, beyond compare.
Each heartbeat sings a timeless tune,
Binding our spirits like the moon.

From ashes rise, like phoenixes soar,
In every ending, there's a door.
Beyond the dark, the light will gleam,
Echoes of faith, living the dream.

With every step, the path unfolds,
Resilient hearts are brave and bold.
In unity, we stand, we fight,
Echoes of life, our guiding light.

A Meadow of Whimsical Certainty

In fields of green, where flowers sway,
Colors burst forth, brightening the day.
Every petal, a whimsical dance,
In the breeze, they take a chance.

Butterflies flit with delicate grace,
Nature's beauty in every space.
Through laughter and joy, the mood is bright,
A meadow alive, pure delight.

The sky drapes low, a canvas fair,
Clouds drift softly, a gentle air.
With every moment, certainty grows,
In this haven, life overflows.

Time holds still in this enchanted place,
A sanctuary of warmth and grace.
Whimsical dreams, like ribbons unfurled,
Painting the edges of our world.

With every heartbeat, magic weaves,
In every corner, possibility breathes.
In the meadow, where dreams take flight,
Whimsical certainty shines bright.

The Bookmark of Belief

In pages worn by time and care,
Lies a story, waiting to share.
With gentle hands, we turn the leaves,
In every chapter, our heart believes.

The bookmark rests, a silent guide,
Through twists and turns, it won't hide.
Each word a step, each line a chance,
In the dance of fate, we advance.

With ink that flows like rivers wide,
Every tale a journey, a trusted ride.
Underneath the cover, magic swirls,
In the depths of the book, the world unfurls.

As stories breathe life, we're intertwined,
With dreams to cherish and hearts defined.
The bookmark of belief stays strong,
In this timeless saga, we belong.

With every turn, a truth revealed,
Through love and loss, we are healed.
In every narrative, we find our worth,
The bookmark of belief shows our birth.

Gardens of Faith

In the dawn's gentle light, seeds we sow,
Roots entwined in dreams, watching them grow.
Petals whisper softly, courage to ignite,
In the gardens of faith, where shadows take flight.

Each blossom a promise, every hue a prayer,
Among the lush greenery, love lingers there.
Tendrils of hope, reaching high above,
In the gardens of faith, we nurture our love.

Through trials and storms, we cultivate grace,
With hands that are weathered, yet hearts interlace.
In the soil of our souls, where truth starts to bloom,
In the gardens of faith, we banish the gloom.

Seasons will change; yet, steadfast we stand,
Guided by the light of a divine, gentle hand.
In silence, we gather, our spirits embrace,
In the gardens of faith, we find our true place.

With every small victory, we rise and we shine,
Together in unity, our paths intertwine.
In the gardens of faith, with each step we take,
We thrive in this beauty, for love's sacred sake.

A Trust Built on Silence

In the quiet moments, we find our way,
A bond unspoken, where hearts gently sway.
In the still of the night, voices remain,
A trust built on silence, neither loss nor gain.

Eyes that meet softly, a language so pure,
In the warmth of your gaze, my soul finds its cure.
No words need to linger, our thoughts intertwine,
In the trust built on silence, your heart is a sign.

The world may be noisy, with chaos around,
Yet in our still haven, true solace is found.
With gestures so tender, we nurture the flame,
In the trust built on silence, we honor the same.

Through seasons of change, through storm and through
sun,
A whisper of comfort, in silence, we've won.
When the chaos encroaches, we will stand as one,
In the trust built on silence, our love has begun.

Let the world keep its chatter, its doubts and its fears,
In the calm of our hearts, we'll wash away tears.
In the trust built on silence, forever we'll stand,
Two souls intertwining, in love hand in hand.

Waves of Belief

On shores of conviction, our spirits collide,
With waves of belief, we embrace the high tide.
Every crest that arises, a tale to unfold,
In the ocean of hope, where dreams are of gold.

With each ebb and flow, we grow ever strong,
In harmony's rhythm, where we both belong.
The chorus of whispers, the dance of the sea,
In the waves of belief, we find you and me.

Castles of wishes, built firm in the sand,
Waves wash them gently, but together we stand.
Holding tight to each other, we brave every storm,
In the waves of belief, our hearts keep us warm.

As the sun greets the dawn, painting skies anew,
In the language of faith, we know what is true.
The tides may keep changing, yet we will stay free,
In the waves of belief, it's just you and me.

Through tempests and trials, we'll sail boldly forth,
With hope as our compass, wherever it's worth.
In the waves of belief, we'll forever set sail,
Together through life, we will always prevail.

The Pulse of Peace

In the heart's gentle rhythm, we find our repose,
The pulse of peace whispers, where soft breezes blow.
In the hush of the twilight, our spirits unite,
In the pulse of peace, all is calm and right.

Like the rustle of leaves, in a warm summer breeze,
The pulse of peace beckons, inviting with ease.
In moments of stillness, we share in the glow,
With each beat of peace, our love starts to grow.

In the canvas of night, where stars brightly gleam,
The pulse of peace cradles each cherished dream.
With the moon as our witness, we dance through the dark,

In the pulse of peace, we've ignited a spark.

Through trials we navigate, with courage aligned,
The pulse of peace pulses, a bond intertwined.
In the depths of our hearts, we find solace and cheer,
In the pulse of peace, we have nothing to fear.

As the dawn breaks anew, we embrace every chance,
With faith as our anchor, we'll savor this dance.
In the pulse of peace, our souls truly soar,
In love's endless rhythm, forever and more.

Treasures of Silent Companionship

In the stillness, hearts abide,
Unspoken words, side by side.
A glance, a touch, our bond grows,
In silent depths, true love glows.

Moments shared, both vast and small,
In quiet times, we find our call.
Hand in hand, through shadows cast,
A treasure found, forever vast.

Through laughter's echo, joy remains,
In whispered dreams, love unchains.
Together, in the evening light,
With silent grace, our souls take flight.

In solitude, we feel the thread,
That weaves our lives, where paths have led.
A tapestry of trust unfolds,
As warmth and peace our hearts enfold.

In every silence, a promise stays,
In every pause, the heart conveys.
Together we stand, life's gentle sway,
In treasures found, come what may.

The Ease of Gentle Surrender

In tender moments, we release,
Letting go brings our hearts peace.
With every breath, a weight is shed,
In gentle waves, our fears are led.

Like autumn leaves, we drift and fall,
Embracing change, we heed the call.
In soft surrender's warm embrace,
We find ourselves in tranquil grace.

The current flows, we let it be,
In open hearts, we find the key.
With every step, a trust we gain,
In gentle ease, we break the chain.

With every heartbeat, we align,
In the rhythm divine, we twine.
Letting life unfold its way,
In surrender's ease, we choose to stay.

Together in the ebb and flow,
We cherish all that we can know.
In gentle tides, our spirits blend,
With every moment, we transcend.

A Lighthouse in the Fog

Amidst the haze, a beacon bright,
Guides weary souls through murky night.
With steadfast beams that pierce the gray,
A lighthouse stands, to light the way.

The waves may crash, the storm may howl,
Yet in its glow, our fears disavow.
In every flicker, hope ignites,
A promise kept through shadowed nights.

Upon the shore, where dreams may drift,
The lighthouse offers a guiding gift.
In foggy realms, we find our ground,
In its embrace, lost hearts are found.

Through trials faced, and tempests churned,
The flame within forever burned.
With courage drawn from distant shores,
We navigate through shifting moors.

As dawn breaks forth, the fog retreats,
The lighthouse fades, yet love repeats.
In every journey, come what may,
Its light remains to guide our way.

The Palette of Quiet Harmonies

In gentle tones, the colors blend,
Soft melodies that never end.
With every brush, a whisper finds,
An artful dance of heart and minds.

The hues of life in tender strokes,
In silence woven, the spirit yokes.
Each note released, in quiet time,
Creates a canvas, pure and sublime.

With every shade, emotions sway,
In tranquil moments, we drift away.
A symphony of subtle grace,
In quiet harmonies, we embrace.

The brush of dusk, the dawn's sweet light,
In every layer, the shadows fight.
Through gentle rhythms that bring us peace,
The palette dwells where echoes cease.

In artful tunes, our souls align,
In whispered songs, a love divine.
Together, in this quiet stream,
We find the strength to softly dream.

A Refuge of Steadfast Hearts

In whispers soft, we find our home,
A harbor safe where we can roam.
With every glance, a promise made,
In steadfast love, we are not afraid.

Through stormy nights and sunny days,
Our bond will shine in countless ways.
Within these walls, the world feels right,
Together, we embrace the light.

With heartbeats like a gentle drum,
In silence shared, we know we're one.
Though trials come, we brave the fight,
In unity, we find our might.

Through every laugh and every tear,
In cherished moments, we draw near.
This refuge built with love's own art,
A timeless dance of steadfast hearts.

So hand in hand, we journey forth,
Each step we take reveals our worth.
In love's embrace, we found our part,
Forever bound, dear steadfast hearts.

The Comfort of Shared Moments

A cup of tea on rainy days,
The warmth of smiles in gentle ways.
In laughter shared, we find our peace,
A simple joy that will not cease.

Watching sunsets, fingers twined,
In moments past, our hearts aligned.
With stories told and secrets spun,
Together, we are always one.

In quiet nights, we share our dreams,
In whispered hopes, our future gleams.
The dance of time, a sweet embrace,
In simple things, we find our place.

Though life may change and seasons shift,
Our bond remains a cherished gift.
Through every trial, every start,
We find the joy that fills the heart.

So let us linger, just a while,
In comfort found in every smile.
For in each moment, love resides,
In shared delights, our bliss abides.

Hidden Shores of Reliability

In shadows deep where secrets lie,
A steady hand to lift the sky.
Like ancient trees that stand so tall,
In whispered trust, we'll never fall.

Through shifting sands and tides that churn,
In every lesson, we will learn.
The beacon bright, a guiding light,
In hidden shores, we find our sight.

Though paths grow rough and dreams may wane,
In every struggle, there's no pain.
A bond so strong, it won't betray,
Together, we embrace the day.

The roots we share run deep and wide,
In love's embrace, we will abide.
Through storms we weather, come what may,
In every heartbeat, find our way.

So here we stand, through thick and thin,
On hidden shores, our lives begin.
For in this trust, we rise, we soar,
In reliability, forevermore.

When Stars Align in Unison

In twilight's glow, the heavens sing,
A cosmic dance, our souls take wing.
When paths converge in fateful grace,
We journey forth, our hearts embrace.

With every star that lights the night,
In harmony, we share our light.
In whispered dreams, our hopes collide,
Together, we become the tide.

In moments shared, the world feels right,
An endless sky, a wondrous sight.
As constellations guide our way,
In unity, we'll never stray.

Though shadows loom and doubts may creep,
In faith and love, our promise keeps.
With every heartbeat synchronized,
In stellar bonds, we're mesmerized.

So let us dance beneath the stars,
In fateful nights, our dreams are ours.
When stars align, the universe shows,
In unison, our love just grows.

The Unfurling of Souls

In the quiet of dawn's first light,
Hearts begin their gentle flight.
Whispers of dreams take their form,
While shadows retreat from the warm.

Each layer sheds, revealing grace,
In tender moments, we find our place.
A dance of fears, a step towards trust,
In the unfurling, we rise, we must.

The journey is steep but oh, so wise,
Through trials, we learn to rise.
Hands intertwine, a sacred bond,
As love teaches us to respond.

In the depths, the truths unfold,
Stories of courage silently told.
From fragile seeds, we grow anew,
Life's canvas painted in vibrant hue.

In this ballet of heart and soul,
We weave the pieces to become whole.
Together we sail the winds of change,
In unity, we break the strange.

Echoes of Reliability

In shadows cast by dusky lights,
There lies a strength in silent fights.
Promises made in the dark of night,
Are the echoes that guide our flight.

Through storms that whisper doubt and fear,
We cling to truths that draw us near.
In steady hands, we find our ground,
Within the heart, where hope is found.

The world may tremble, but we stand firm,
With roots that sink, we won't squirm.
Each vow a stone, each word a flame,
In the dance of trust, there's no shame.

In laughter shared and tears that flow,
Through every ebb, together we grow.
A symphony of hearts entwined,
In mutual grace, our souls aligned.

So here we'll rise, with heads held high,
In moments shared, we won't deny.
The echoes ring in the heart's own core,
With every beat, we long for more.

Tides of Comfort

In whispers soft, the tides do call,
A gentle pull, we rise, we fall.
The moonlight dances on the sea,
Bringing forth a calm melody.

In soothing waves, our worries fade,
With each embrace, fear is laid.
Together we drift, lost in the night,
Finding refuge in starlit light.

The depth of the ocean holds our dreams,
In flowing currents, hope redeems.
When storms arise, we find our way,
In the heart of the tide, we'll stay.

The ebb and flow, a rhythmic grace,
In unity, we find our place.
With every surge, we recognize,
In the sea of warmth, love never dies.

So let the waters soothe your soul,
In every crest, we are made whole.
Tides of comfort, ever near,
In our togetherness, there's no fear.

The Strength in Stillness

In the hush of a tranquil dawn,
Time seems to sip its gentle brawn.
With every breath, a moment grows,
In stillness, the heart learns to know.

The world rushes by, in frantic chase,
Yet in quietude, we find our space.
A deepened breath, a calming sigh,
In moments slow, we learn to fly.

Amidst the chaos, a steady stream,
In the silence, we find our dream.
The fortress built on peace so pure,
In stillness, we find strength to endure.

Close your eyes, feel the ground anew,
In the pause, let your spirit break through.
The earth beneath, so firm, so sure,
In the quiet, our souls endure.

So take a moment, breathe it in,
In stillness, we find where we begin.
With every heartbeat, let love swell,
In the strength of silence, we dwell.

A Dance in Still Waters

In the night, whispers flow,
Beneath the stars that gently glow.
Ripples trace the surface clear,
As shadows dance, drawing near.

A breeze hums soft, a tender song,
The oaks sway, the night is long.
Rippling dreams upon the lake,
Where silence holds, and hearts awake.

Moonlight spills on liquid glass,
Each moment sweet, as seasons pass.
Nature's breath, a sacred pause,
In this realm, we find our cause.

Time suspends, in twirling grace,
Night's embrace, our sacred space.
With every sway, a promise grows,
In still waters, love bestows.

Let us dance, two souls entwined,
Where echoes of the heart remind.
In every ripple, a story told,
A dance in stillness, forever bold.

The Heart's Silent Promise

In a glance, a truth unspoken,
Words unneeded, vows unbroken.
Each heartbeat sings a quiet tune,
In shadows cast by a silver moon.

Soft whispers brush against the air,
Promises linger, love laid bare.
In every pause, a longing sigh,
Boundless dreams that never die.

Through trials faced, and paths unknown,
Our hearts entwined, forever grown.
In silent moments, trust is built,
A foundation formed without guilt.

With every dawn, hope's light unfolds,
In warm embraces, stories told.
The heart's soft song will always stay,
A silent promise, come what may.

Through storms we'll sail, through skies so gray,
Together strong, we'll find our way.
In the silence, love will bloom,
In every heartbeat, a sacred room.

Cradled by the Moonlit Tide

Underneath the starlit sky,
The ocean whispers, soft and high.
Waves embrace with tender grace,
Cradled dreams in this sacred space.

Moonlight spills upon the shore,
Suspended moments, we explore.
Each wave a promise of the night,
Guiding us to hearts' delight.

Footprints trace the sands of time,
In twilight's glow, our souls align.
Cradled by waves, our spirits soar,
In this embrace, we ask for more.

Time stands still, in ebb and flow,
The tide reveals what hearts may know.
In lullabies of night and tide,
Love's gentle journey, side by side.

As stars reflect on water's face,
We find our peace, our rightful place.
Cradled by the moonlit tide,
With every wave, our hearts abide.

Echoes of Unspoken Bonds

In silent glances, words retreat,
An understanding, bittersweet.
Between the notes, a music plays,
In quiet hearts, the truth conveys.

The space between, a sacred trust,
In every moment, love is just.
Unseen connections, deeply felt,
In tender hands, emotions melt.

Reflection in the softest gaze,
A dance of souls, a timeless maze.
Echoes linger, soft and low,
In every heartbeat, love will grow.

When shadows fall, we stand aligned,
In whispered prayers, our spirits bind.
Every silence speaks so clear,
A bond unbroken, always near.

Through the chaos, through the night,
Together, we will find the light.
In echoes sweet, our promises tread,
In unspoken bonds, love's thread.

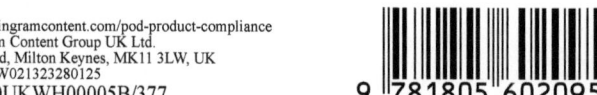